I CAN SPELL!

Turn the wheel at the back of the book to see the different letters. Then find the right letter to complete the name of the objects on each page. You will know it is the right one when the colours match.

Campbell Books

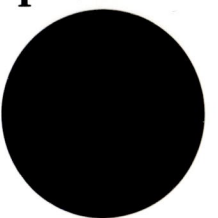

He is warm and fluffy.

Think of a nice name for him.

c ● t

You can keep things in this.

What would you put in it?

b●x

He lives on the farm.

What other animals live on the farm?

p●g

Some children go to school in this.

How do you go to school?

b●s

She lays eggs for us.

Draw some brown speckled eggs.

h●n

This is full of milk for breakfast.

What do you like for breakfast?

j●g

You can carry your shopping in this.

Which shop do you like best?

b ● g

Baby wears this at meal times.

Why does baby need it?

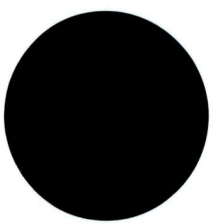

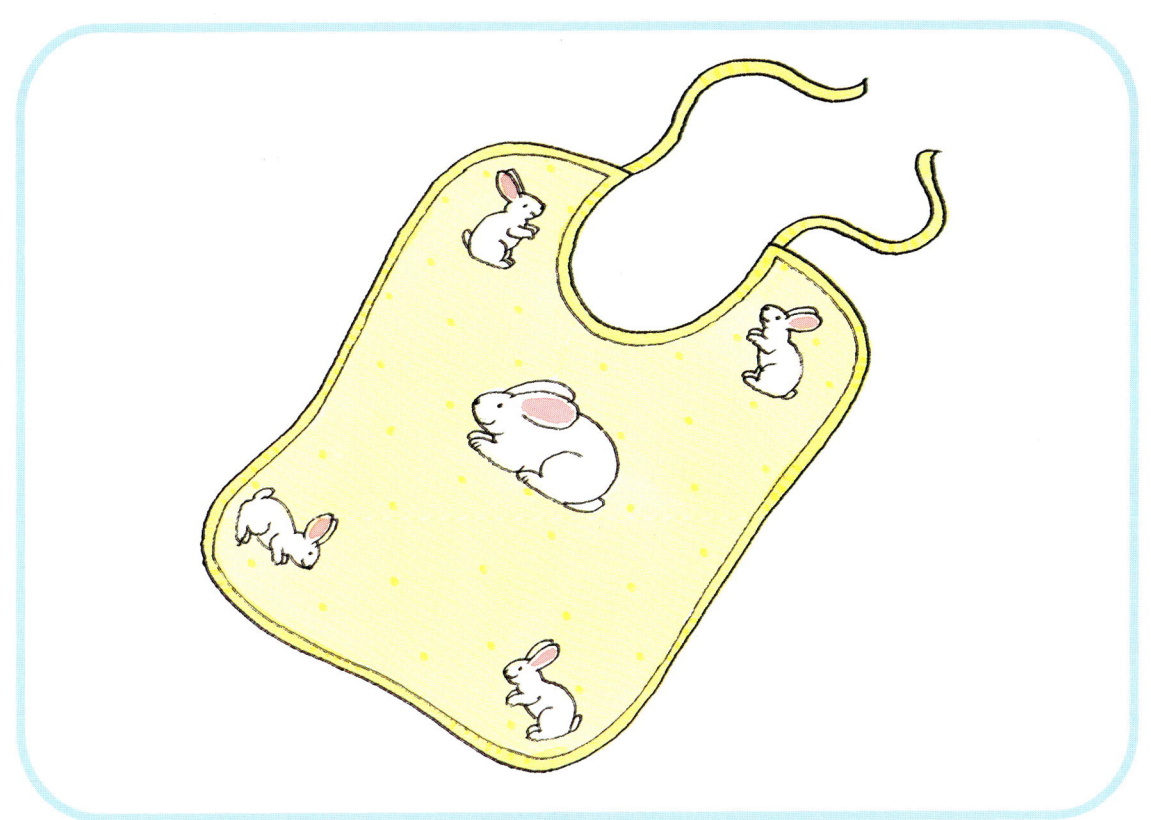

b●b

You shake this to make it ring.

Have you seen one like this?

b●ll

You put this on your head.

What else can you wear on your head?

h ● t

She barks and wags her tail.

What else can she do?

d●g

© Rod Campbell 1987
First published 1987 by Octopus Books Ltd
This edition published 1994 by
Campbell Books
12 Half Moon Court · London EC1A 7HE
All rights reserved

Printed in Singapore
ISBN 1 85292 171 4